SUMMER COOKING

MARGARET ROBERTS HERB SERIES

Summer Cooking with Herbs

Illustrated by
Sanmarie Harms

David Bateman

© Margaret Roberts 1986

Originally published by Lowry Publishers.
This edition published in 1988 by David Bateman Ltd,
'Golden Heights', 32–34 View Road, Glenfield,
Auckland 10, New Zealand

Reprinted 1989
Reprinted 1992

ISBN 1 86953 015 2

A David Bateman book
Printed in Hong Kong by Colorcraft

Contents

Introduction

Many countries have long, hot summers which are tiring and make the preparing and eating of meals a huge effort. Too frequently we tend to settle for packaged and quickly prepared foods. These in turn fail to give us the 'fuel' we need to combat the heat and stress of our urban lives – and so the pattern continues. A proper diet is essential if we are to aim for peak fitness and efficiency in our daily work. We need top-grade 'fuel' in our systems to keep us fit, strong and on top of things, for if there is no joy in our step, no song in our hearts, and no pleasure in our menus, what is life all about? Eating right, thinking right, means living right and that is the aim of this little book – to offer and encourage a new way of eating, and perhaps a new perspective on life.

The recipes here are all old favourites and, like good friends, have stood the test of time and have given pleasure to all who have tried them. Personally, I always prefer to follow quick and easy recipes and this book is for those people who, like me, have little time to spend preparing meals in the kitchen, even though they may enjoy cooking. A summer diet should include plenty of fresh salads and uncooked food and emphasis has been laid on this aspect in preparing these recipes.

My thanks go to those of my friends who tasted and enjoyed each dish, putting their seal of approval on the recipes. Thanks also to Sanmarie Harms, a wonderful friend and artist, to Kathy Marais for her typing and ability to put into order my excited outpourings, and to June Jackson for her ever-present help, encouragement and enthusiasm. Finally, my thanks to Alison Lowry, my editor, who put it all together with neat, farsighted thoroughness. I appreciate you all.

Should you need any assistance, or if you have a query, I am sure your local health food or herb shop will help.

May this little book open up new tastes and pleasure for all who work with it.

A Bouquet of Summer Herbs

Herbs can put magic into an ordinary dish. They can change the taste with strong or subtle flavouring and make a meal an experience. Listed here is a collection of easily available herbs, all of which can be grown in a window-box or in a small patch of garden. Try to grow your own herbs if possible; it will make all the difference to your meals, and will give you an interest and delight in the garden.

ANGELICA (*Angelica archangelica*)

Used mostly for confectionery and flavouring, angelica is a most attractive plant in the garden. Crystallised angelica stems are used for decorating cakes and puddings on special occasions. The leaves can be used to make a pleasant tea, and a little chopped stem – 60 ml (¼ cup) herb to 250 ml (1 cup) boiling water – is an excellent tea for the digestion, bringing swift relief from flatulence and colic.

Raw stalks chopped into a little cream cheese and spread onto biscuits makes a tasty after dinner snack.

BASIL (*Ocimum basilicum*)

Basil makes a particularly delicious addition to tomato dishes, and adds a strong and exciting flavour to salads and fish dishes. It also has remarkable medicinal properties, being a tonic, antiseptic and digestive herb. Leaves mixed into salad oil will help relieve constipation and it is used to stimulate perspiration and thus bring down a temperature. In the summer months, therefore, when basil flourishes (it is an annual), take full advantage of it and use it as a cooling herb.

Basil vinegar and basil cooking oil are two ways of adding a special flavour to a dish.

BAY (*Laurus nobilis*)

Midsummer is when bay is at its flavour-filled best. I stuff bay leaves inside a chicken when planning to use it cold, and it can be used in sauces, marinades and pickles. The longer bay is cooked, the better the flavour. Remove the leaves after cooking, however, or they will become bitter. Bay is an important ingredient in the classic *bouquet garni*, which should contain: 2 sprigs parsley, 2 sprigs chervil, 1 sprig marjoram, 1 sprig thyme, and 2 bay leaves. Tie into small bags and use either fresh or dried.

BERGAMOT (*Monarda didyma*)

This is an old-fashioned perennial. Its attractive red flowers are prolific from midsummer onwards. It makes a delicious tea and used as a base for fruit drinks, bergamot is hard to beat. To combat heat exhaustion *bergamot milk* will soothe and relax:

12,5 ml (1 heaped tbsp) fresh bergamot leaves, chopped
250 ml (1 cup) boiled milk
little honey to sweeten

Pour the boiled milk over the bergamot and allow to stand for 10 minutes. Strain, then sweeten with honey. Drink it while still warm, preferably just before going to bed.

5

BORAGE (*Borago officinalis*)

Borage is a quick growing summer annual. Its beautiful blue flowers make an unusual addition to fruit salads and the leaves, finely chopped and added to salads, impart a cucumber-like taste and coolness. The leaves can be added to wine and claret cups, not only for their cool flavour, but because borage is known as the 'herb of gladness', and is said to dispel depression and exhaustion – nature's own 'pep pill'.

CELERY (*Apium graveolens*)

Here is a vitamin-packed, mineral salt-filled bunch of energy. Celery is particularly important in the summer months for cleansing and flushing the body – through the urine – of waste matter.

Celery leaves are reported to contain certain hormones which have an effect similar to insulin, and invalids, diabetics and anyone on a salt-free diet will benefit enormously from celery in the diet. Celery stimulates the digestion, has a toning effect on the glandular system and relieves rheumatism and gout. Chop green, fresh celery into salads and you will find its rich, meaty taste will make it a favourite with everyone. Celery tea is excellent for heat fatigue, as a diuretic and as a cure for kidney and bladder infections.

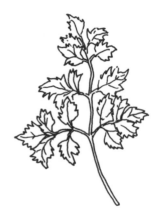

CHERVIL (*Anthriscus cerefolium*)

The delicate flavouring of this herb is best appreciated in soups and sauces. Chervil is blood cleansing and diuretic and has a stimulating effect on the glandular system. Easily grown as a summer crop (it needs midsummer shade), it can be used as a garnish, chopped into salads, sprinkled over roasts and added to cream cheese for spreading on sandwiches. As it cools the body, it will bring down a fever and increase perspiration, making it a valuable addition to the diet in hot weather.

CHIVES (*Allium schoenoprasum*)

Chives are part of the onion family and as such have mild antibiotic properties. Their pleasant taste makes them an ideal garnish and they are delicious in salads. Chives in the diet have a beneficial effect on the kidneys and help lower blood pressure. They are also a digestive aid. Chives are particularly good in egg dishes, cheese dishes and fish dishes.

DANDELION (*Taraxacum officinale*)

The dandelion is a weed, and not very welcome in the garden; yet it has such high nutritional value that it should be included in the diet, particularly in spring and early summer. It is a blood cleanser, a tonic and plays an important role in regulating the functioning of the gall-bladder. Its diuretic and digestive qualities make it a valuable herb and it can be eaten daily in salads or added to stews and soups. Take care to choose young, tender leaves as the herb is somewhat bitter.

COMFREY (*Symphytum officinale*)

Comfrey is an important herb in the diet and its vigorous summer growth ensures its availability for several months. Choose young leaves for including in salads; the older leaves can be chopped for fritters, dipped in batter and fried, or used in green drinks and soups. It is bland, milky and has a cucumber-like taste, and can be mixed with other herbs. Excellent as an aid to healing broken bones, sprains, bruises, arthritis, chest conditions, and eye conditions, comfrey is a valuable addition to the herb garden.

DILL (*Peucedanum graveolens*)

A rather special, delicate herb for flavouring, dill is a great favourite all over the world. Excellent in aiding digestive processes, it relieves colic, flatulence and stomach spasms. Chew dill seeds to combat halitosis and stay hunger pains. Dill in the diet of nursing mothers is excellent for stimulating milk production. The health-giving mineral salts contained in dill give it its reputation of being good for the whole system and it particularly benefits people on a salt-free diet. Use chopped leaves sprinkled over salads, fish and poultry dishes.

ELDER (*Sambucus nigra*)

In summer the elder tree is a profusion of honey-scented flowers. Not only are they health giving and delicious in champagne and in cakes, puddings and fritters, but they have wonderful medicinal properties as well. Used in cosmetics, elder flowers are cleansing and healing, and taken as a tea they are both sedative and relaxing, especially in the summer's heat. Elder flowers in the bath will soothe, cleanse and soften the skin, particularly if you are suffering from sunburn.

FENNEL (*Foeniculum vulgare*)

Related to dill, fennel is also a favourite flavouring for fish dishes. At the same time it has anti-flatulent, anti-colic and calming properties. It will also sweeten the breath and aid digestion. Particularly good with fish, fennel helps digest fats and its liquorice-like flavour adds subtly to sauces and dressings. Fennel leaves and the shaved root bulb are diuretic, and fennel seed tea is a favourite with weight watchers. Fennel grows very easily and should always have a place in the garden.

GARLIC (*Allium sativum*)

Pungent and strong, garlic is perhaps the best-known flavouring herb. Just a touch is all that is needed – a mere wiping of a bowl with a garlic clove and the taste is there. Garlic is a natural antibiotic, and is particularly good for chest conditions, infections and rheumatism. It is a tonic herb and has long been used to build up the body against infection. Chew a sprig of parsley after eating garlic to sweeten and clear the breath. In meat, fish and savoury dishes, garlic can either be cooked or finely chopped and used raw, sprinkled over the cooked dish. I find garlic vinegar is excellent in salad dressings for a true appreciation of its flavour.

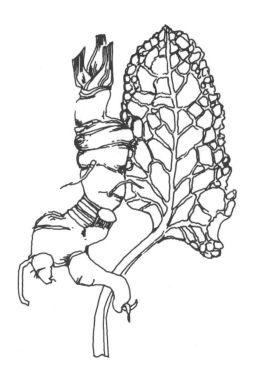

HORSE-RADISH (*Cochleria armoracia*)

Horse-radish root has a hot, pungent flavour but is cooling at the same time. This makes it not only an excellent flavouring but a healthy addition to the diet. It has antiseptic and anti-biotic properties and contains substances hostile to bacteria – therefore horse-radish is useful in preserving food and in cleansing the intestines. Fresh, raw horse-radish, grated on a slice of buttered brown bread, is greatly beneficial in the treatment of cystisis, and bladder and kidney ailments. It helps the liver function and has a strong diuretic effect. It also makes an excellent seasoning for diabetics and for people on special diets. Grated fresh root can be added to sauces and dressings, salads and steamed vegetables.

LAVENDER (*Lavendula officinalis*)

The beautiful fragrant lavender is particularly cooling in summer drinks and fruit puddings. The flowers and leaves, which calm and soothe, lifting headaches and aiding sleep, can be used to make a tea which in turn is added to fruit juice, jellies or honey for a calming effect after a hectic day. Lavender has a singular taste and it relieves colic and flatulence. It can also be added to vinegar for salad dressings and to sugar and jellies for a different and pleasant taste.

LAVENDER SUGAR

500 ml (2 cups) sugar
125–250 ml (¹/₂ – 1 cup) fresh lavender flowers and leaves

Mix the lavender and sugar by shaking together in a screw-top jar. Leave for a week, shaking up every day for a few minutes. Use in tea or coffee or to sweeten fruit salads and drinks.

LEMON BALM (*Melissa officinalis*)

Lemon balm must be amongst the most loved of summer herbs. It is refreshing in fruit drinks, makes a wonderful iced tea, gives a fresh lemony taste to ice-cream, fruit puddings and cakes, and its calming, cooling and restorative properties make it essential for the summer diet.

It aids perspiration, thus bringing down a fever, and gives relief from nausea, anxiety and stomach-aches. Strong lemon balm tea is not only uplifting and calming but it can also be used in a water solution as a face-wash or in the bath.

LEMON THYME (*Thymus citriodorus*)

Similar in properties to its close cousin, *Thymus vulgaris*, lemon thyme can be used in sweet dishes and puddings, drinks and wines. A few sprigs cooked with stewed fruit adds a delicious fragrance and flavour. Remove before serving.

LEMON VERBENA (*Lippia citriodora*)

Lemon verbena enhances sweet dishes and summer drinks with a pure, rich lemon taste. Made into a tea, then cooled and added to fruit drinks, it is delightfully refreshing.

Used to flavour jellies and ice-creams, lemon verbena is a favourite with everyone. It also aids digestion, nausea, flatulence, vomiting and depression. Very young leaves, finely chopped, can be sprinkled into cakes, puddings and fruit salads.

LUCERNE (*Medicago sativa*)

For its strengthening and invigorating properties, lucerne is essential in your summer diet. Fresh young leaves chopped into salads are a delicious ingredient. Sprouted seeds can be used in soups and on sandwiches. Primarily lucerne restores energy and tones the body. It improves the functioning of the kidneys and, because it is a neutraliser, it soothes acid indigestion. It is a fine herb for sportsmen and for those who lack energy and stamina, particularly when it is heat induced. Lucerne tea can be added to fruit juice for a quick pick-me-up.

MARJORAM (*Origanum majorana*)

Not only is marjoram distinctive in its delicious flavour, but it has disinfecting and preserving qualities as well, one of the reasons why it is added to preserved sausages, meat patés and aspics. It stimulates the digestive juices, thus aiding digestion, and it is also believed to increase the white blood corpuscles, speeding the healing of infections. Marjoram improves the circulation, clears mouth infections and, used externally as a poultice, heals bruises and wounds. Either fresh or dried, its flavour enriches all savoury dishes and it particularly enhances egg and poultry dishes.

MINT (*Mentha* varieties)

Summertime is the time for the mints. Refreshing in drinks, salads, fruit dishes and as a tea, mint is unsurpassed in its fresh flavour. Chew a sprig of mint and you will be surprised how it will revive you even on the hottest day. Mint is excellent for relieving flatulence, colic, liverishness and nausea. It clears gall-bladder tension and rheumatic aches and pains. Altogether, it is a wonderful toning and reviving herb and all through summer's heat it should be used generously.

NASTURTIUM (*Tropaeolum majus*)

Nasturtium is another antibiotic herb. Fresh leaves and flowers contain vitamin C and in some countries it is used as a sort of herbal penicillin. To clear up throat infections, coughs and colds, simply eat a few nasturtium leaves. It is a pleasant substitute for pepper and the flowers add piquancy and colour to a salad. If you have a stomach ulcer, nasturtium adds a peppery taste to bland foods but will not harm the ulcer. Pickled nasturtium seeds add relish to salads and savoury dishes as a substitute for capers, and chopped leaves, in small amounts, make a delicious addition to salads, especially mixed into potato salad.

PARSLEY (*Petroselinum crispum*)

Possibly the most used of all herbs, parsley is rich in vitamins A, B and C. It is anti-flatulent, digestive, cleansing, toning, cooling and anti-spasmodic. It improves the working and tone of the entire body and for this reason should regularly be included in the diet.

Particularly effective in summer, parsley is diuretic and cooling. Fresh chopped parsley, sprinkled on all savoury dishes, will keep you fit and full of energy. When used in cooking parsley should be added at the last moment to preserve all its goodness.

ROSE-SCENTED GERANIUM (*Pelargonium graveolens*)

Sweet scented and sweet tasting, scented geraniums add delicacy of flavour to fruit puddings, jellies, milk puddings and ice-cream. They also impart calming, soothing and relaxing qualities – a freshly picked bowl next to your bed will ensure a good night's rest in the midsummer heat. Put a leaf or two in a finger bowl on the table when serving fruit and the water will be beautifully fragrant; take a bath with a sprig of geranium in the water at the end of a long, hot day and see how relaxing it is. Use a leaf to seal a jar of jam or add a few leaves when cooking a sweet dish. Scented geranium leaves are in fact perfect in all sweet dishes.

ROSEMARY (*Rosmarinus officinalis*)

Not only is rosemary a flavour-filled herb, used in sweet and savoury dishes, but it is also full of health-giving goodness. A good digestive aid, it also relieves flatulence, stimulates the circulation, and combats tiredness, nervousness, tension, headaches and anxiety. Rosemary can be used to make a tea, which can be drunk hot or cold; it can be chopped into salads and added to all sorts of dishes. Its reputation for stimulating hair growth is well founded, and a cup of rosemary tea first thing on a summer morning will set you up for the rest of the day.

Dried rosemary twigs burned on a barbecue give a special taste to mutton chops and sausages, and used in stuffings and marinades, rosemary is a firm favourite.

SAGE (*Salvia officinalis*)

The health-giving properties of sage are legend. Strong and pungent, sage is a fine tonic and brings relief to many complaints – colds, coughs, chest conditions, fevers, rheumatism, memory loss, circulation, indigestion, colic, sore throats, and mouth infections! Used in making drinks, it can also be chopped into savoury dishes, and a leaf or two chewed every now and then will clear up many ailments. Add a little freshly chopped sage to savoury dishes in the last moments of cooking to ensure that it retains all its goodness. Sage tea added to fruit juice is a refreshing summer drink. Combine sage with cheese and pasta dishes for a different flavour.

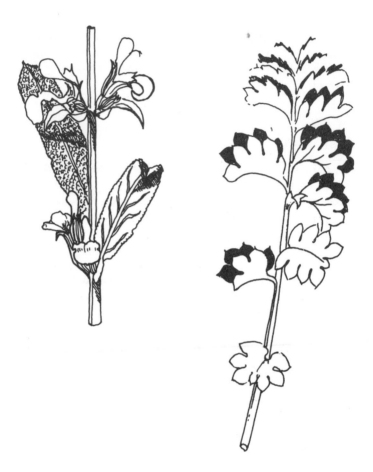

SALAD BURNET (*Sanguisorba officinalis*)

Always vigorous and green in the garden, salad burnet makes a pleasing addition to summer salads and cold soups. It is a tonic, cooling herb. The wild cucumber flavour enhances salads and it is decorative sprinkled over savoury dishes just before serving. Stir chopped, fresh leaves into mayonnaise and salad dressings, dips and sauces. It is a most refreshing and reviving herb.

SORREL (*Rumex acetosa*)

The sour, acidic taste of sorrel enhances both salads and fish dishes. Sorrel soup is a favourite in French cuisine. As this herb has amazing healing properties for conditions such as kidney stones, fevers, liver ailments, bladder infections, and blood conditions, it should be incorporated into the diet often. Too strong and acid a taste to be eaten alone, a little sorrel in a salad is delicious, and chopped, fresh sorrel sprinkled over cream cheese, cold cream soups and fish dishes brings out the best in this useful herb.

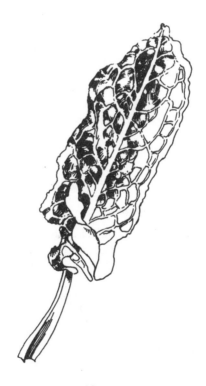

STRAWBERRY (*Frageria vesca*)

Because of its wonderful medicinal properties, the strawberry is considered to be a most valuable addition to the garden. During the brief season, eat all the strawberries you can as they act as a tonic, a blood cleanser, a revitaliser, a muscle toner and a nerve fortifier. For over-copious menstruation, diarrhoea, and skin ailments such as eczema and heat rash, strawberries are a well-known treatment. A chilled bowl of fresh strawberries in midsummer is remarkably cooling as they are refrigerant and have the ability to bring down fevers. Include this fruit in fruit salads, in making drinks and in puddings.

TARRAGON (*Artemisia dracunculoides*)

Tarragon has a subtle flavour, and is excellent in vinegars, as well as sprinkled onto roasts, poultry dishes and salads. It soothes digestion and cools the circulation. Do not cook tarragon as it then loses its flavour. Add fresh and finely chopped to the dish when serving. Add it to dips and sauces and use it lavishly.

THYME (*Thymus vulgaris*)

Thyme is an astringent and cleansing herb – excellent for relieving flatulence and indigestion, as well as for sore throats, colds and depression. It has sedative and calming properties and it also deodorises and cleanses breath, and disinfects. Strongly flavoured, thyme is an appetising ingredient in most savoury dishes – meat, fish, cheese, poultry and pasta. Chopped and sprinkled lightly onto salads, roasts and breads, its rich flavour enhances every dish. Dried thyme stalks should be saved and burned on a barbecue to add flavour to the meat.

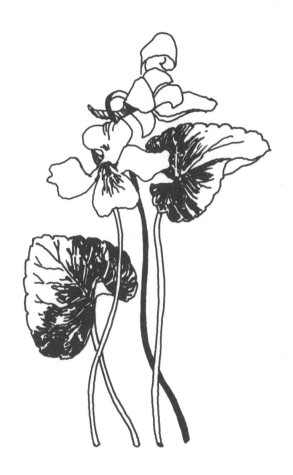

VIOLET (*Viola odorata*)

The violet is one of nature's most powerful dissolvents. Used for the treatment of stones, swollen glands, boils, coughs or colds, violets will also dissolve phlegm, strengthen the heart and dispel headaches. Violet flowers and chopped leaves can be made into teas or added to salads. The flowers can be crystallised and added to ice-cream and milk puddings, milkshakes and fruit salads.

WATERCRESS (*Nasturtium officinalis*)

Watercress flourishes in pure running water in summer and it is a much loved salad herb. It has the amazing properties of toning and cleansing the blood, aiding anaemia and soothing rheumatic aches and pains. It improves the eyesight, strengthens the nerves and the heart, and it helps dissolve tumours, swellings and cysts. Include watercress in salads, and eat it on sandwiches and with savoury dishes.

Soups

Summer soups need to be chilled and light. They can make a cooling start to a meal or, served with homemade biscuits, crusty bread or a finger of pie, they are enough for a meal. Add the herbs at the last moment, fresh and green if possible, or half the specified quantity if using dried herbs.

HERB STOCK FOR SUMMER SOUPS

1 cup herbs (eg parsley, celery, mint, basil, chives, lucerne, or a combination)
1–2 litres (4–8 cups) boiling water
1 onion, chopped
little salt
20 ml (4 tsp) debittered yeast or meat extract

Pour boiling water over herbs and chopped onion. Stand, then add the meat or yeast extract and a little salt. Strain when cool.

This stock can be used as a base for making a healthy, quick, uncooked summer soup. Add 250 ml (1 cup) chopped cucumber, 250 ml (1 cup) chopped lettuce, 250 ml (1 cup) chopped watercress, 250 ml (1 cup) chopped tomato, and blend in a liquidiser. A cup of yoghurt, or 125 ml (½ cup) sour cream will change the texture, and by varying the amount of water you can find your own consistency.

Sorrel, tarragon, borage and salad burnet are also delicious when liquidised into the base stock. Try liquidising avocado, adding a little lemon juice, into the stock, with watercress or sorrel. This makes another rich and satisfying soup.

Experiment with this cool soup and you will find it supremely satisfying. Garnish with chopped parsley, chervil or salad burnet to make a party dish.

CHILLED BEETROOT SOUP (Serves 10)

6 beetroots (large)
3 litres (12 cups) chicken or herb stock
500 ml (2 cups) yoghurt
250 ml (1 cup) sour cream
250 ml (1 cup) chopped celery
250 ml (1 cup) chopped dill
juice of 1–2 lemons
salt and pepper to taste

Grate beetroots and boil up in chicken or herb stock for 10 minutes. Set aside to cool, then put through a liquidiser. In a bowl blend yoghurt, sour cream, chopped herbs, salt and pepper. Chill. Just before serving blend in the liquidised beetroot and stock, lemon juice and the yoghurt and herb mixture. Serve chilled with a sprinkling of chopped dill.

SORREL SOUP (Serves 6–8)

1 large head lettuce, finely chopped
250–500 ml (1–2 cups) chopped fresh sorrel
4 potatoes, peeled and chopped
1 onion, chopped
salt and pepper to taste
250 ml (1 cup) fresh spinach
2–3 litres (8–12 cups) stock or water
37,5 ml (3 tbsp) fresh chervil or parsley
25 ml (2 tbsp) butter

Sauté the chopped onion and spinach in the butter. Add sorrel
and lettuce and sauté. Add potatoes, stock and seasoning.
Simmer gently for 30 minutes. Liquidise and serve hot or cold,
sprinkling a little chopped chervil or parsley on top of each
soup bowl. This is a favourite soup in France. In order to make
it more substantial it can be served over a slice of hot buttered
toast. I have found that a topping of grated cheese adds to the
flavour.

CHILLED CUCUMBER AND FENNEL SOUP
(Serves 4–6)

1 peeled cucumber, coarsely chopped
25–50 ml (2–4 tbsp) chopped fennel leaves and stalks
8 spring onions (leaves too), chopped
125 ml (½ cup) chopped chives
juice of 1 large lemon
1 litre (4 cups) iced water
250 ml (1 cup) cream or 250–500 ml (1–2 cups) yoghurt (plain)
salt and freshly ground pepper to taste

Liquidise the cucumber, fennel, spring onions, lemon juice and a little of the water. Stir in the cream or yoghurt, and salt and pepper. Add enough of the chilled water to make a pouring consistency. Pour into individual bowls, garnish with chopped chives and a little chopped, fresh fennel. Serve with croûtons.

VICHYSSOISE WITH SUMMER HERBS (Serves 6–10)

This traditional creamy, cold soup with some garden fresh herbs added to it is a winner and a favourite with everyone. Serve it for supper on a hot night with herb scones as a side dish. Follow with watermelon balls and mint and the meal is guaranteed of success.

6 leeks, finely chopped
2 onions, finely chopped
37,5 ml (3 tbsp) butter or oil
1 litre (4 cups) chicken stock
4 potatoes, peeled and thinly sliced
salt and freshly ground black pepper to taste
1 litre (4 cups) milk
2 ml (½ tsp) paprika
250 ml (1 cup) heavy cream
125 ml (½ cup) chopped celery
125 ml (½ cup) chopped borage
125 ml (½ cup) chopped chives

Sauté onions and leeks in the butter or oil. Cover and cook, but do not brown. Add stock, potatoes, salt and pepper. Cook until all the vegetables are tender. Add herbs. Cook for one minute, then liquidise, or put through a sieve. Heat the milk and the cream and add to the vegetable mixture. Beat well. Chill. Serve very cold, topped with a sprinkling of chopped chives.

COLD TOMATO SOUP WITH BASIL (Serves 6–8)

6 large tomatoes, chopped
50 ml (4 tbsp) chopped onions
37,5 ml (3 tbsp) chopped tarragon
37,5 ml (3 tbsp) brown sugar
10 ml (2 tsp) salt
freshly ground black pepper
250 ml (1 cup) chopped chives
60–125 ml (¼–½ cup) chopped sweet basil
250 ml (1 cup) sour cream

Purée the tomatoes, basil, tarragon, onions and half the chives.
Stir in the sugar, salt and pepper and sour cream. Chill. Serve
with a sprinkling of chives in individual bowls.

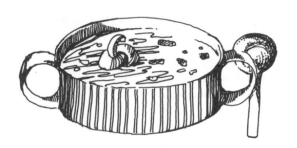

GREEN SUMMER SOUP (Serves 10)

3 litres (12 cups) strong stock (chicken or beef)
750 ml (3 cups) chopped spinach
3–4 cups mixed greens: salad burnet, outer leaves of lettuce,
*   borage leaves, comfrey leaves*
250 ml (1 cup) chopped green onions
37,5 ml (3 tbsp) chopped tarragon
500 ml (2 cups) chopped celery
500 ml (2 cups) finely grated carrots and a few chopped carrot tops
*   (½ cup)*
125 ml (½ cup) chopped parsley
25 ml (2 tbsp) butter
50 ml (4 tbsp) flour
salt and pepper to taste
250 ml (1 cup) fresh cream or yoghurt

Sauté the chopped onions, celery and carrots in the butter. Add the stock, salt and pepper, spinach, and the mixed greens. Simmer for 10–15 minutes. Liquidise. Take 250 ml (1 cup) of the soup and stir in the flour. Return the soup to the pot, add the flour mixture and stir until thickened. Stir in cream. Serve either hot or cold with a sprinkling of chives and tarragon.

Fish
Dishes

Fish not only makes a nourishing meal, but is extremely good for you, and during summer can be served as a cool, refreshing dish. Fish can be prepared in many ways. I often buy double the quantity I need so that I can marinate half of it. I prepare either raw or grilled fish in a marinade and leave it in the refrigerator overnight. As the marinades can vary, I never tire of fish dishes.

Herbs that go well with fish are fennel, dill, basil, bay, chervil, garlic, horse-radish, marjoram, sage, thyme, sorrel, tarragon and watercress – a large selection, giving wonderful scope for experimenting. Instead of merely frying fish, try spicing egg or flour or breadcrumbs with herbs (I find dried herbs work best) to coat the fish before cooking it. I make a special fish blend that I keep separately in a screw-top jar.

FISH SPICE

125 ml (½ cup) freshly ground black pepper
125 ml (½ cup) freshly ground coriander seeds
125 ml (½ cup) freshly ground fennel seeds
125 ml (½ cup) freshly ground celery seeds
125–500 ml (½–1 cup) dried tarragon

Mix well by shaking ingredients together in a screw-top jar. Label and date the jar. When preparing breadcrumbs or flour to dip fish into before frying, blend in a teaspoon or two of this fish spice. You will find it makes all the difference.

HORSE-RADISH FISH SPICE (Enough for 6)

This is one way of giving a different taste to fried fish. In this instance I have found grated fresh horse-radish root, blended with melted butter, to be tastier than dried, although horse-radish preserved in vinegar, drained, can also be delicious.

50 ml (4 tbsp) grated horse-radish
37,5 ml (3 tbsp) butter
2 garlic cloves, crushed and chopped
salt and pepper to taste
12,5 ml (1 tbsp) chopped fennel or dill leaves
12,5 ml (1 tbsp) chopped parsley

Melt the butter, and add the salt, pepper and herbs. Pour over the fish and grill.

MARINADE FOR RAW FISH

50 ml (4 tbsp) sunflower oil
1 onion, thinly sliced and chopped
2 garlic cloves, finely chopped
juice of 1 large lemon or 2 small lemons
10 ml (2 tsp) thyme
6 crushed allspice berries
little black pepper
5 ml (1 tsp) salt
12,5 ml (1 tbsp) honey
5–10 ml (1–2 tsp) mustard

Put all the ingredients into a screw-top jar. Shake well. Cut thin fillets of raw fish, lay them in a shallow dish and pour the marinade over them. Keep in the refrigerator for 4–6 hours, turning every now and then. Grill the fish fillets lightly, basting with the marinade.

MARINADE FOR GRILLED OR FRIED FISH

Once the fish has been fried or grilled in your normal way, a new and exciting taste can be given by marinating the freshly fried or grilled fish. Place fish pieces in a shallow dish, and pour the marinade over them (a basic one is given on p 35). Place in the refrigerator, turning every now and then, and keep refrigerated for 3–5 hours. Serve chilled with a salad.

BASIC MARINADE (Enough for 6)

(Change the herbs to suit your own particular taste)

50 ml (4 tbsp) oil
1 dessertspoon dried mustard
25 ml (2 tbsp) Worcestershire sauce
12,5 ml (1 tbsp) thyme
12,5 ml (1 tbsp) finely chopped celery
12,5 ml (1 tbsp) finely chopped dill or fennel
25–50 ml (2–4 tbsp) lemon juice or tarragon vinegar
1 bay leaf, crushed
3 garlic cloves, crushed
a twist or two of finely peeled lemon peel
little salt and pepper

Place all ingredients in a screw-top jar and shake well. Pour over fried or grilled fish. Leave in refrigerator for 3–5 hours, basting from time to time.

FISH PATE

Paté is a delicious way of serving fish. It is best served with slices of toast, or on herb scones, and with a salad it makes an appetising lunch dish. I usually make double the quantity and freeze what is left over.

1 glass white wine
5 ml (1 tsp) freshly ground black pepper
1 bay leaf
12,5 ml (1 tbsp) chopped celery (leaves and stalk)
12,5 ml (1 tbsp) chopped chives
2 onions, finely chopped
250 ml (1 cup) water

Boil all ingredients together for about 15–20 minutes in a covered pot. Strain.

300 g (12 oz) haddock (or smoked haddock) or cod (or smoked cod),
or a combination of both
225 g (8 oz) butter
12,5 ml (1 tbsp) flour
150 ml (½ pt) cream
juice of 1 lemon
salt and pepper to taste
250 ml (1 cup) chopped fennel leaves

Melt a little of the butter and cook the fish in it. Keep the pot covered. When cooked, flake the fish. Melt 50 g (2 oz) of butter, stir in the flour and add the stock, a little at a time, until a smooth sauce forms. Add the flaked fish and season. Press into a buttered paté dish or 2 or 3 individual dishes. Sprinkle with fennel, pat down well, and pour over the rest of the melted butter to seal it. Keep refrigerated.

FISH SALAD (Serves 6)

This is a quick and easy summer meal. Served with breadrolls, it is satisfying and delicious. Thinly sliced fennel and cucumber can be used instead of apple or tomato.

1 tin tuna
2 apples, grated
125 ml (½ cup) chopped celery, leaves and stalks
6 ml (½ tbsp) chopped marjoram
2 tomatoes, chopped
250 ml (1 cup) cooked brown rice
250 ml (1 cup) mayonnaise
125 ml (½ cup) chopped chives
juice of 1 lemon
freshly ground black pepper
little salt
250 ml (1 cup) grated pineapple (optional)
chopped parsley

Flake the tuna. Blend all the ingredients and serve chilled in a glass bowl. Sprinkle with parsley.

PICKLED FISH

This is a typical pickled fish recipe and far easier to make than it sounds. Served cold with salads, it is hard to beat on a hot day. White-fleshed fish are best for pickling, but most others can be used in this recipe.

3–4 kg raw fish, filleted and cleaned
6 large onions, thickly sliced
salt and freshly ground black pepper
3 bay leaves, crushed
few peppercorns and allspice berries
juice of 2 lemons
125 ml (½ cup) curry powder
250 ml (1 cup) brown sugar
5 cups brown vinegar
12,5 ml (1 tbsp) thyme, finely chopped
6 ml (½ tbsp) sage, finely chopped

Cut slices of fish, sprinkle with salt and pepper and fry in oil until cooked. In the meantime, mix all the other ingredients and boil up together in a covered pot. Remove the bay leaves. Place pieces of fish into a deep dish and pour the hot sauce over them. Alternate fish and sauce layers until all ingredients are used up. Cover and leave to cool. Place in refrigerator overnight to enable the sauce to saturate the fish. Serve with salad.

BAKED SOLE AND ROSEMARY (Serves 6)

6 soles (or flounders)
6 sprigs rosemary
juice of 2 lemons
salt and pepper to taste
25 ml (2 tsp) butter
6 pieces tinfoil

Trim and wipe the soles. Lay each sole on a square of tinfoil. Sprinkle both sides with a little salt and pepper and lemon juice. Dot with butter, lay a rosemary sprig on top of each sole and fold up the tinfoil. Place on a baking sheet and bake at 180°C/350°F for 20–30 minutes. Just before the cooking time is up open the tinfoil and brown the soles under the griller. Serve with a green salad.

Meat Dishes

Cold meats make particularly nourishing summertime meals. They usually need a stronger flavouring and seasoning than meat which is served hot. Thyme, bay, marjoram and oregano help to preserve meat, a good tip for midsummer heat.

SUMMER HAM

1,5 kg (3 lb) pickled forehock pork or gammon
  (order from your butcher in advance)
2 bay leaves
little rum
6 peppercorns
1 peeled pineapple, thickly sliced
100 g (4 oz) brown sugar
cloves

Cover the salted pork or gammon in unsalted water. Bring to the boil. Throw out the water and boil again in fresh water to which the bay leaves and peppercorns have been added. Allow 15 minutes per 500 g (1 lb) in weight. Drain, peel off the skin, and score the fat into diamond shapes. Press a clove into the centre of each diamond. Place in a baking dish. Sprinkle with the sugar and arrange the pineapple pieces around the meat. Pour a little rum over the meat and the pineapple and bake for ½–1 hour at 180°C/350°F, basting occasionally. Check every now and then to make sure that it does not burn. Allow to cool, then keep refrigerated. Serve thin slices with salads. Any leftover slices can be used in the next recipe.

HAM IN HERB JELLY (Serves 6)

4 cups chopped ham
250 ml (1 cup) fresh parsley, chopped
250 ml (1 cup) chopped chives
250 ml (1 cup) green cooked peas
1 chopped tomato, medium sized
125 ml (½ cup) chopped celery
12,5 ml (1 tbsp) oregano
500 ml (2 cups) boiling water
10 g gelatine

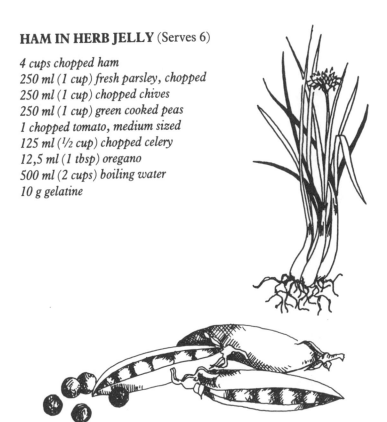

Pour the boiling water over the gelatine and stir well. Add the parsley. (If you prefer a lot of jelly, double the quantity of gelatine and water.) Mix all the other ingredients and season lightly. Stir in the gelatine and parsley mixture, pour into a loaf-shaped dish and refrigerate immediately. When set, turn out onto a flat dish and garnish with parsley and hard-boiled egg slices.

Any cold cut can be used in this way, eg mutton, beef or veal, and it is always a favourite. It keeps well and makes an excellent standby for unexpected weekend guests.

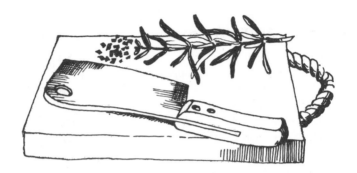

COLD BAKED SILVERSIDE

Unfortunately silverside is often overlooked as a special occasion dish. Delicious cold, it can form a base for supper or lunch, needing only a few salads to make a satisfying and tempting meal. Whatever size of piece you choose it can be prepared in the same way.

corned beef
2 or 3 carrots, peeled, or
2 or 3 onions, thickly sliced
2 garlic cloves, crushed
3 bay leaves
peppercorns
sprig of thyme or rosemary

Before cooking the corned beef soak it in water for about 2 hours. Then place the beef in a deep ovenproof pot. Surround it with carrots or onions, the garlic cloves, bay leaves, a few peppercorns and a sprig or two of thyme or rosemary. Fill the pot with water and cover closely. Place on a low shelf in the oven and bake at low to medium heat for 3–4 hours. Then test to see if it is tender (take care not to over-cook as it will crumble). Drain the beef from the liquid, place it on a plate and cover with greaseproof paper. Allow to cool, and then keep refrigerated. Serve with mustard or horse-radish sauce and assorted salads.

KEBABS

Delicious at a barbecue, kebabs can be prepared a day or two in advance. They are always a great success.

leg of mutton, cut into cubes – approx 1,5 kg (3lb) meat
lemon leaves
salt and pepper to taste
1 onion, sliced
1 garlic clove, crushed
brown sugar
125–250 ml (½–1 cup) milk

Line a deep dish with lemon leaves. Sprinkle salt and pepper over the mutton cubes and place them in the dish, alternating with slices of onion and a little crushed garlic. Sprinkle with a little brown sugar and pour the milk over the meat. Cover with lemon leaves and place in the refrigerator overnight.

Marinade

50 ml (4 tbsp) apricot jam
25 ml (2 tbsp) brown sugar
50 ml (4 tbsp) curry powder
3 bay leaves
12,5 ml (1 tbsp) fresh lemon thyme leaves (or 6 ml (½ tbsp) dry lemon thyme)
2 ml (½ tsp) salt
4–6 peppercorns
juice of 2 lemons
125 ml (½ cup) vinegar

Thread the cubes of meat on skewers alternately with small onions. Lay them in a shallow dish, pour the marinade over them, and leave to stand overnight in the refrigerator. Barbecue them the following day and serve with salads and freshly baked bread.

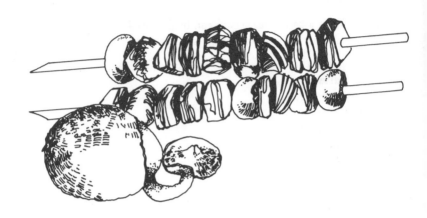

BEEF CURRY (Serves 6)

A traditional curry dish that can be served either hot or cold. I find it a wonderful standby as it can be prepared in quantity and frozen. It keeps well too and is a favourite with everyone. Try serving it with cold potato and tomato salad, and crusty bread rolls, for Sunday lunch on a hot day.

1 kg (2½ lb) lean minced beef
1 thick slice brown bread
250 ml (1 cup) full cream milk
37,5 ml (3 tbsp) cooking oil
25 ml (2 tbsp) apricot jam
juice of 2 lemons
10 lemon leaves
2 onions, finely chopped
25 ml (2 tbsp) curry powder
25 ml (2 tbsp) brown sugar
2 eggs, well beaten
5 ml (1 tsp) salt
125 ml (½ cup) seedless raisins, soaked overnight in water
freshly ground black pepper
6 dried peaches, soaked overnight in water
12,5 ml (1 tbsp) fresh oregano, or 6 ml (½ tbsp) dried

Fry the onions in the oil. Soak the bread in the milk and when soft squeeze out the milk and set aside. Mix the meat, bread and the chopped, soft peaches, raisins and the jam with the onions. Blend the curry powder, lemon juice, sugar, salt and pepper and the oregano. Add to the meat mixture. Spoon into a fairly shallow baking dish. Beat the eggs and milk in which the bread was soaked and pour over the meat. Press in the lemon leaves, submerging half of them at regular intervals. Bake for approximately 45 minutes at 180°C (375°F) or until browned. Serve with rice, coconut, chutney and mango slices.

COLD POT-ROAST TOPSIDE

This is an old-fashioned way of making a mouthwatering roast. You will need a heavy-bottomed pot or casserole that can be used on top of the stove; it must have a good fitting lid. This dish needs to cook slowly to preserve its juices and richness. The aroma alone is enough to give the most jaded of palates a lift. I usually find it more economic to cook a large piece; as a cold meat it offers many varieties in serving.

approx 1,75 kg (4 lb) topside corner cut
6–10 garlic cloves
25 ml (2 tbsp) chopped, fresh sage
juice of 2 lemons
black pepper
15 ml (3 tsp) salt
4 onions, medium sized
500 g (1 lb) fatty bacon
little grated nutmeg
cooking oil

With a sharp knife make incisions in the meat at regular intervals, about 10 in all. Push a piece of bacon into each incision and on top of it a peeled garlic clove. Heat the oil in the heavy-bottomed pot and place the meat in it. Arrange the sliced onions all around the meat. Pour the lemon juice over the meat, sprinkle with salt and pepper, and the sage and a dash of nutmeg. Brown the meat on all sides. When richly browned, add 500 ml–1 litre (2–4 cups) water and a sprig of fresh sage. Reduce the heat, cover and simmer gently. Check from time to time that the meat is not sticking and turn it over so that all sides are cooked evenly. Cook for about 2 hours or until the meat is tender (most of the gravy will have boiled away). Serve either hot with salads or drain off the gravy (use for stock) and refrigerate. Slice when cold and serve with salads and mustard.

Poultry Dishes

Everybody loves a good roast chicken and for the long, hot summer days it is a wonderful standby. I often roast two chickens together, one for eating hot and the other for eating cold, either set into aspic or served with a herb dressing.

COLD CHICKEN IN HERB SAUCE

1,5 kg (3½ lb) chicken, roasted and carved into fairly small pieces

Herb Sauce

250 ml (1 cup) yoghurt
juice of 1 lemon
125 ml (½ cup) chopped dill
12,5 ml (1 tbsp) chopped parsley
12,5 ml (1 tbsp) chopped celery
25 ml (2 tbsp) honey
25 ml (2 tbsp) oil
50 ml (4 tbsp) mayonnaise
little salt and pepper

Blend all ingredients. Pour over the chicken pieces. Refrigerate. Decorate with watercress before serving.

CHICKEN IN ASPIC (Serves 10)

For this recipe I like to boil the chicken, or roast it in a little water in a clay pot in the oven, so that I can use the chicken gravy, which jellies when it cools, as the base for the aspic.

1 chicken, 1,5 – 1,75 kg (3½–4 lb), cut into small pieces
20 g (2 envelopes) gelatine
1 litre (4 cups) liquid, made up of chicken gravy or vegetable or
  herb stock
little salt and pepper
2 hard-boiled eggs
10 ml (2 tsp) chopped, fresh marjoram
25 ml (2 tbsp) mint leaves

Warm 250 ml (1 cup) of the liquid and stir in the gelatine. Mix until it is dissolved, then add the rest of the liquid. Lightly butter a loaf tin or ovenproof loaf-shaped dish. Arrange the hard-boiled eggs in a neat pattern along the bottom. Pour in a little of the stock and gelatine mixture, then place the cut up chicken pieces into the mould. If you have a few leftover green peas or cooked carrot rings, use these to decorate the sides of the loaf. When all the pieces are in place, pour over the remaining liquid, tuck the mint leaves down the sides, cover and place immediately in the refrigerator. When set, turn out of mould and serve sliced with salads.

TURKEY MAYONNAISE WITH BASIL (Serves 6)

Leftover turkey from Christmas festivities can be used for this delicious recipe. Simple to make, it is adaptable for turkey, duck or chicken. I usually plan on one cup of chopped turkey pieces per person.

6 cups chopped turkey
250–500 ml (1–2 cups) mayonnaise
250 ml (1 cup) chopped celery
37,5 ml (3 tbsp) chopped parsley
salt and pepper to taste
little lemon juice
25 ml (2 tbsp) chopped, fresh sweet basil

Blend all the ingredients. Serve cold with salads.

CHICKEN BARBECUED WITH HERBS (Serves 8–10)

On a summer evening this is an easy and mouthwatering way
to serve chicken.

12 chicken pieces
12 pieces tinfoil, approximately 20 cm square

Sauce

190 ml (¾ cup) brown sugar
250 ml (1 cup) vinegar
125 ml (½ cup) chopped parsley
125 ml (½ cup) chopped lovage
12,5 ml (2 tbsp) curry powder
salt and lemon pepper to taste
12 nasturtium leaves and flowers, chopped

Blend all the ingredients. Place the chicken pieces in a bowl,
and pour the sauce over them. Cover and place in the refrigerator for 2–3 hours, turning every now and then to make sure
each piece is well covered. Remove chicken pieces and place
each one on a square of tinfoil. Spoon a little sauce over each
piece, wrap tightly in the tinfoil, and place on the hot coals of
the fire. Barbecue for approximately 15–20 minutes, turning over
once or twice. Serve with sweetcorn and a rice salad.

COLD DUCK WITH TARRAGON

Cold duck makes a tasty change for a summer dinner. For me, duck is at its best cold and served simply with freshly baked bread.

1 duck
little oil
10 sprigs tarragon
125 ml (½ cup) tarragon vinegar
2 onions, roughly chopped
3 carrots, roughly sliced
125 ml (½ cup) parsley
salt and lemon pepper
250 ml (1 cup) pineapple juice
125 ml (½ cup) honey

Heat the oil in a casserole and brown the duck on all sides. Tuck the onion and carrot and tarragon sprigs all round the duck. Mix together the vinegar, pineapple juice and honey and pour over the duck. Sprinkle with salt and pepper and cover. Place in a moderate oven, 180°C (350°F), and roast for 1–1½ hours or until the duck is tender. Baste from time to time with the juices. Cool. Serve sliced with salads and fresh bread. Save the dripping to spread on bread, or for stock.

Vegetable
Dishes

Summer vegetables are so varied and abundant that your menus need never be dull or repetitive. Try experimenting on your own to vary the dishes even further. In all of these recipes you can substitute several different vegetables.

SALADS

For me this heading encompasses anything fresh that is served either combined or alone with a dressing. The list below is intended to suggest a few unusual and flavour-filled combinations to start you off. Throughout I have used summer's best vegetables, all used raw and thus wonderfully healthy.

Grated fresh beetroot and apple, with chopped chervil.

Grated butternut squash with grated pineapple and chopped tarragon.

Sliced cucumbers with tomato and basil.

Sliced courgettes with celery and yoghurt.

Chopped dandelion greens with lettuce, cucumber and marjoram.

Chopped borage with grated carrots and pineapple.

Salad burnet with nasturtium leaves and flowers and grated carrots.

Chopped chives with cream cheese and cucumber slices.

Finely chopped comfrey with sliced tomato and chopped basil.

Chopped celery with young uncooked corn kernels, sliced from the cob, and lettuce.

Finely sliced fennel and pineapple with chervil.

Chopped spinach greens, with chopped mint and pineapple.

Chopped oregano with grated apple and watercress.

Chopped sorrel with sliced cucumber and dill.

Watercress with hard-boiled eggs and chopped thyme.

Chopped greens, eg lettuce, borage, dandelion leaves, spinach, celery and chives with grated cheese.

Grated radishes and tarragon with grated apple.

Sliced green peppers, chopped lovage and tomatoes.

Sliced mushrooms, thyme and courgettes.

Lettuce, sliced radishes, nasturtium flowers and leaves.

All of these salads need a dressing. A basic dressing can be found on page 65. Again try combinations until you find one that pleases you.

POTATO SALAD (Serves 6–8)

Potato salad is perhaps the best known of all salads. You can
vary it by adding different herbs or making mayonnaises. This
is a basic potato salad recipe and a wonderful standby.

6 potatoes, boiled in their jackets
500–750 ml (2–3 cups) mayonnaise
125 ml (½ cup) chopped parsley
125 ml (½ cup) chopped celery
12,5 ml (1 tbsp) chopped fennel
salad burnet or chervil for decoration
salt and freshly ground black pepper

Peel and slice the potatoes when cold. Mix celery, fennel and
parsley with the mayonnaise. Sprinkle the potatoes with the
salt and pepper and carefully fold in the mayonnaise mixture.
Spoon into a bowl and decorate with chervil or salad burnet.
Serve cold.

TABOULEH

This is a delicious traditional Arabian wheat salad.

500 g (1 lb) wheat
750 ml (3 cups) salted water
250 ml (1 cup) chopped chives
250 ml (1 cup) chopped mint
125–250 ml (½–1 cup) salad oil
1 clove garlic, finely minced
125–250 ml (½–1 cup) tarragon vinegar
125 ml (½ cup) brown sugar
12,5 ml (1 tbsp) thyme (or oregano or marjoram)

Soak the wheat overnight in water. The next day drain it, and boil it up for 5 minutes in the salted water. Drain and cool.

Mix together the salad oil, garlic, tarragon vinegar, brown sugar and thyme. Combine all ingredients and serve cold as a salad.

COURGETTES AND THYME

450 g (1 lb) courgettes
25 g (1 oz) butter
30 ml (2 tbsp) finely chopped thyme
juice of ½ lemon

Grate the courgettes coarsely. Melt the butter in a large pan and stir-fry the courgettes and the thyme. Stir until the grated courgettes begin to soften (about 2 minutes), then sprinkle with lemon juice. Stir in well. Serve hot. A more substantial supper dish can be made by adding:

250 ml (1 cup) chopped mozarella cheese
30 ml (2 tbsp) chopped chives
125 ml (½ cup) chopped almonds

If served cold, add a little tarragon vinegar. If served hot, grill slightly to soften the cheese.

RED PEPPERS IN BASIL OIL

A summer crop of green peppers can be allowed to ripen to a succulent red. Sliced, skewered and dredged in basil oil, they make a delectable grilled dish, either barbecued or grilled in the oven in a shallow baking dish.

3 garlic cloves, finely chopped
juice of 2 lemons
250 ml (1 cup) cooking oil
500 ml (2 cups) finely chopped basil
salt and freshly ground black pepper
4 large red peppers

Slice peppers into thick strips and remove the seeds. String the strips onto skewers, spacing with onions, olives or cheese squares if desired. Pour over a little oil and grill lightly until the peppers are soft.

Oil

Blend together chopped garlic, basil oil, lemon juice, salt and pepper. Place in a screw-top jar. Shake vigorously. Once the peppers are soft and lightly grilled, place on a bed of lettuce or on thick slices of fresh bread and dribble the rest of the basil oil over them.

GREEN BEAN CURRY

1 kg (2 lb) green beans
3 medium onions, finely chopped
1 dessertspoon mustard powder
1 heaped dessertspoon cornflour
5 ml (1 tsp) turmeric
12,5 ml (1 tbsp) chopped rosemary
500 ml (2 cups) brown sugar
250 ml (1 cup) tarragon or rosemary vinegar
1 dessertspoon curry powder
10 ml (2 tsp) salt

Slice the green beans. Boil together with chopped onions until soft. Drain. Mix all the other ingredients, add to the bean and onion mixture and bring to the boil. Simmer gently for 15 minutes. Bottle, or keep in the refrigerator and serve with cold meat, fish or poultry.

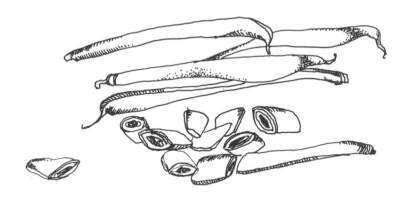

SWEETCORN GRILL WITH MINT

During the sweetcorn season, take every opportunity to include them in your diet. Corn on the cob at a barbecue makes a memorable meal.

6 freshly picked corn on the cob
12 sprigs mint
75 ml (6 tbsp) butter cut into 12 equal pieces
big pot of cold water to which 125–250 ml (½–1 cup)
  salt has been added

Carefully peel back the husks from the corn without detaching them, and remove the silk. Tuck 2 mint sprigs and 2 pieces of butter into each and pull up the husk, fully encasing the corn. Soak in the salted water for about an hour. Drain and place them on hot coals, turning frequently for 10–15 minutes. The wet husks will steam as the cobs cook and they will not dry out.

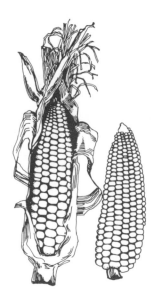

SWEETCORN BREAD

6 corn on the cob, cooked and stripped off
2 eggs, beaten
12,5 ml (1 tbsp) sugar
2 ml (½ tsp) salt
6–12,5 ml (½–1 tbsp) chopped rosemary or mint
1 dessertspoon baking powder
125–250 ml (½–1 cup) milk

Whisk all ingredients and mix in the sweetcorn. Place in a greased bowl and cover with tinfoil securely held in place. Stand in a pot of boiling water and steam for 2 hours. Remove from the mould, slice and spread with butter. This bread can be served as a vegetable or as a snack.

Sauces and Accompaniments

Ordinary dishes can take on exciting new flavours by the addition of a variety of sauces or dressings. Once again these are some basic recipes, all of which can be adjusted, using different herbs to suit your own taste.

YOGHURT DRESSING

Excellent as a salad dressing or as a dip – particularly useful for dieters and those on a low fat diet.

250 ml (1 cup) plain yoghurt
12,5 ml (1 tbsp) lemon juice
37,5 ml (3 tbsp) chopped chives (or garlic, or onion)
12,5 ml (1 tbsp) chopped sweet basil (or oregano, or marjoram, or lovage)
cayenne pepper
little salt
2 ml (½ tsp) allspice

Whisk all ingredients together, adding the herbs last of all. I find fresh herbs are best for this dressing.

MAYONNAISE

Mayonnaise is the traditional salad dressing used all over the world. These two recipes are basic, one a sweet mayonnaise and the other a standard one. Add herbs of your choice and use lavishly with salads.

(1) SWEET MAYONNAISE

250 ml (1 cup) sweetened condensed milk
125 ml (1/2 cup) vinegar
1 ml (1/2 tsp) salt
125 ml (1/2 cup) salad oil
10 ml (2 tsp) mustard
freshly ground black pepper
2 ml (1/2 tsp) paprika
1 egg yolk, well beaten

Whisk all ingredients together. Pour into a screw-top jar and keep in the refrigerator.

(2) STANDARD MAYONNAISE

1 large egg yolk or 2 small egg yolks
250 ml (1 cup) salad oil
60–125 ml (1/4–1/2 cup) lemon juice
6 ml (1/2 tbsp) mustard

All ingredients must be of the same temperature. Whisk the egg yolk in a liquidiser. Add oil, a few drops only at a time, whisking continuously. Add a little lemon juice, a few drops at a time, until the mayonnaise is thick enough to your taste. Add mustard. Whisk. Spoon into a jar and keep in the refrigerator. Any of the following herbs can be chopped into this mayonnaise, approximately 60–125 ml (1/4–1/2 cup) herbs: basil, fennel, dill, salad burnet, chervil, celery, parsley, marjoram, lovage, oregano, chives, rosemary, sage, tarragon, thyme and mint.

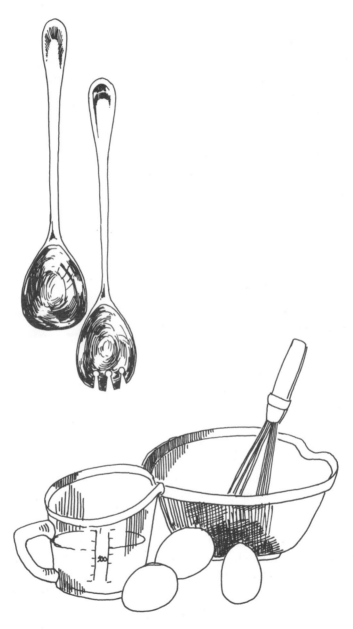

VINEGAR

The piquant taste of herb vinegars enhances all salad dressings. Easily made, no kitchen shelf should be without a variety of herb vinegars and they will please the busy housewife as well as the gourmet cook.

BASIC HERB VINEGAR

1 bottle white wine vinegar
enough fresh herbs to fill the bottle

These herbs are all suitable: rosemary, oregano, thyme, sage, chives, bay, garlic, chillis, parsley, mint, tarragon, marjoram, lovage, nasturtium, salad burnet.

Combinations of herbs are also pleasant. Try some of the following: garlic and chives, parsley and chillis, rosemary and cloves, nasturtium and chives, sage and thyme, bay and oregano, marjoram and mint, salad burnet and lovage.

Stand the bottle in the sun for 3 weeks. During that time change the herbs 3–6 times, depending on the strength of flavour you desire, replacing with fresh herbs each time. Then strain off the vinegar and bottle it. Push in a sprig or two of fresh herb to enable you to identify which vinegar is in which bottle. Use in dressings and marinades.

SPICED VINEGAR

The combination of herbs and spices in this vinegar makes it an excellent marinade as well as an unusual salad dressing. It is particularly good with fish and poultry.

1 bottle brown vinegar
60–125 ml (¼–½ cup) coriander seeds
1 chilli, pricked all over with a needle
250 ml (1 cup) brown sugar
4 bay leaves
6 allspice berries
6 cloves
1–3 cloves garlic, peeled
1 sprig thyme or 10 ml (2 tsp) dried thyme
1 stick cinnamon

Place all ingredients in a pot. Bring to the boil. Remove immediately from the stove. Cool and pour into a dark glass bottle. Cork.

LEMON CREAM DRESSING WITH HERBS

This is a delightful sweet dressing that goes well with fruit tarts, fruit salads, or stewed fruit.

12,5 ml (1 tbsp) lemon juice
2 egg yolks
12,5 ml (1 tbsp) honey
12,5 ml (1 tbsp) fresh, finely chopped mint (or lemon balm, or bergamot, or lemon verbena)
250 ml (1 cup) cream or yoghurt

Whisk the lemon juice with the egg yolks. Add honey. Whip the cream and stir in chopped herbs, blending all ingredients thoroughly. Keep chilled. This sauce is also delicious spread over sponge cake and decorated with fresh strawberries or peach slices.

HEALTH SALAD DRESSING

This is my favourite dressing and one I never get tired of. In my Country Kitchen cooking classes I teach my students to make it and they come up with the most delicious variations. A little of this dressing poured over meat grilling at a barbecue gives it a mouthwatering aroma, and it keeps the meat tender and succulent.

250 ml (1 cup) salad oil
250 ml (1 cup) lemon juice, freshly squeezed
250 ml (1 cup) honey

Pour all three ingredients into a screw-top jar. Seal tightly and shake. Add any of the following herbs, or combinations thereof: 12,5–25 ml (1–2 tbsp) chopped thyme, mint, sage, lovage, marjoram, oregano, basil, chives, garlic, tarragon. Store in the refrigerator and shake each time before using.

TOMATO SPREAD

As tomatoes are abundant in midsummer, this recipe is a summer standard. I serve this spread on squares of homemade bread as a teatime savoury snack.

25 ml (2 tbsp) butter
2 small onions, finely chopped
2 large tomatoes, skinned and chopped
2 ml (½ tsp) salt
little freshly ground black pepper
2 dessertspoons sugar
10 ml (2 tsp) curry powder
2 eggs
12,5 ml (1 tbsp) thyme
12,5 ml (1 tbsp) vinegar

Fry the onions in the butter. Add tomatoes, thyme, salt and pepper, curry powder, and sugar. Stir well until tomatoes and onions are soft. Lastly add beaten egg and stir until the mixture thickens. Cool. When cold stir in the vinegar. Keep in a screw-top jar in the refrigerator. Tomato spread is delicious served with grilled meat or fish, or added to soups and stews.

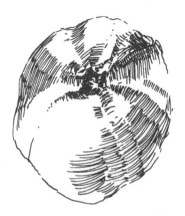

Quick Suppers, Lunches and Snacks

In summer I suspect this section will be the most frequently used. So often one is too hot and tired to bother much with cooking and these recipes keep effort to the minimum. Taking advantage of summer's bounty, you will find these dishes quick and easy and inexpensive.

VEGETABLE KEDGEREE (Serves 6–8)

500 ml (2 cups) cooked rice
3 hard-boiled eggs, chopped (for decoration)
2 cups chopped, mixed greens, eg dandelion leaves, lucerne,
*   borage, watercress, lovage, nasturtium leaves, spinach*
250 ml (1 cup) chopped celery leaves and stalks
250 ml (1 cup) chopped chives
500 ml (2 cups) chopped tomatoes
1 avocado pear, sliced
500 ml (2 cups) green grapes
250 ml (1 cup) chopped cucumber
salt and pepper to taste

Combine all ingredients,
except the eggs. Then
make the dressing.

Dressing

125 ml (½ cup) honey
5 ml (1 tsp) curry powder
125–190 ml (½–¾ cup) salad oil
125 ml (½ cup) herb vinegar, eg tarragon, chive or oregano

Mix ingredients together by shaking in a screw-top jar. If you prefer a more moist salad, double the quantity of dressing. Place vegetables in a salad bowl and carefully mix in the dressing. Decorate with the eggs and serve.

GRILLED STUFFED GREEN PEPPERS (Serves 6)

6 green peppers
500 ml (2 cups) cream cheese
125 ml (1/2 cup) chopped chives
25 ml (2 tbsp) salad oil
5 ml (1 tsp) paprika
1–2 ml (1/4–1/2 tsp) cayenne pepper
salt to taste
1 clove garlic, finely minced
12,5 ml (1 tbsp) fresh, chopped sweet basil
250 ml (1 cup) grated cheddar cheese

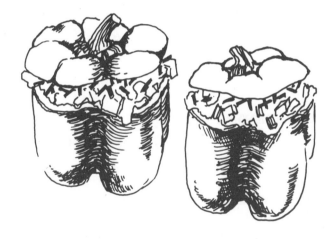

Slice the green peppers in half. Remove the seeds and discard.
Place the peppers on a baking sheet. Mix all the other ingredients except the cheddar cheese. Fill the green peppers
with the mixture. Top each pepper with a sprinkling of grated
cheddar cheese. Bake in a medium oven 180°C (430°F) for 15
minutes or until the peppers are soft. Serve with salads.

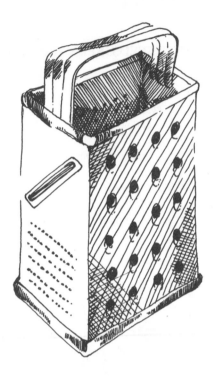

HERBED BREAD FRITTERS (Serves 6)

This is a quick, light and tasty dish requiring very little effort.

6 slices brown bread (trimmed of crusts if desired)
3 eggs, beaten
15 ml (3 tsp) chopped marjoram (or sage, chives, lovage, parsley,
  oregano or basil)
little butter or oil for frying
250 ml (1 cup) grated cheddar cheese
salt and pepper to taste

Blend eggs with salt, pepper, herbs and cheese in a shallow dish. Have ready a pan with hot butter or oil. Coat each slice of bread with the egg mixture and fry it quickly, turning on a spatula to brown both sides. Serve either hot or cold with grilled tomatoes and salad.

TARRAGON EGGS (Serves 6)

This dish can be prepared in advance and left in the refrigerator. It is a cooling, nourishing meal that is wonderfully quick and easy to prepare, and inexpensive.

6 hard-boiled eggs
12,5 ml (1 tbsp) sunflower oil
10 ml (2 tsp) mustard
25 ml (2 tbsp) fresh, chopped tarragon
salt and freshly ground black pepper to taste
37,5 ml (3 tbsp) mayonnaise
chopped parsley
juice of ½ lemon

Shell and halve the eggs, remove the yolks and mash with a fork. Add the oil, mayonnaise and lemon juice, chopped tarragon, salt and pepper. Fill the whites of the eggs with this mixture. Sprinkle with chopped parsley. Serve on lettuce leaves with wedges of tomato and cucumber. For a more festive occasion, make a bed of chopped cucumber, green grapes, rings of green pepper and pickled onions. Arrange the eggs attractively, dot with cheese cubes and pour over a piquant herb sauce.

HERB AND VEGETABLE BAKE (Serves 6)

This is a basic recipe which can be adapted for all sorts of vegetables. It can be served either hot or cold, and it keeps well in the refrigerator. It is particularly good at a barbecue, as it combines well with meat, poultry or fish. It is also tasty just on its own.

3 potatoes, peeled and thinly sliced
6 baby courgettes, sliced
2 onions, chopped
500 ml (2 cups) thinly sliced fennel (bulb and stalks)
250 ml (1 cup) chopped celery (or comfrey or borage)
3 eggs
500–750 ml (2–3 cups) milk
salt and pepper to taste
500 ml (2 cups) grated cheese

Mix all the vegetables and herbs and place in a baking dish. Whisk milk, eggs, salt and pepper. Pour over the vegetables. Sprinkle with grated cheese and bake at 180°C (350°F) for about 1 hour.

Asparagus, pineapple, radish, tomatoes, peas, green beans, turnips, sweet potato and eggplant are all suitable for this recipe. Try adding a little horse-radish or chutney to the vegetables for a different flavour.

Sweets and Puddings

Most countries boast an abundance of summer fruits – strawberries, mulberries, grapes, peaches, melons, apricots, pineapples and pawpaws to name only a few. Nothing is nicer than fresh fruit on a hot day and a fruit salad containing even just a few of the above fruits is always a pleasure. Make your own herb syrup to add to a fruit salad for an unusual taste, either combining herbs or using specific ones. Experiment with those you like best. I find scented geranium leaves, lavender leaves, lemon balm (melissa), mint, lemon verbena and lemon thyme, violets and bergamot are best. Decorate with borage flowers, violets and rose petals.

HERB SYRUP

This makes one cup of syrup which is enough for a large bowl of fruit salad.

125 ml (½ cup) honey or brown sugar
125–190 ml (½–¾ cup) water
1 piece root ginger
1 stick cinnamon
125–250 ml (½–1 cup) herbs

Boil all ingredients together for 8–10 minutes. Cool. Strain. Mix into the fruit salad.

PEACH SORBET (Serves 6)

6 ripe peaches
500 ml (2 cups) sugar
750 ml (3 cups) water
125 ml (½ cup) wine
    (I find sweet white wine the nicest)
5 ml (1 tsp) ground ginger
6 scented geranium leaves or 1 cup bergamot leaves
juice of 1 lemon

Boil up all the ingredients, except the peaches, for 10 minutes. Stand, cool and strain. Meanwhile purée the peaches in a liquidiser. Combine the syrup with the puréed peaches and liquidise again. Pour into an ice cream tray and place in the deep freeze. Stir the sorbet from time to time to break up the crystals. Decorate with a few peach slices and mint leaves, and serve with yoghurt or custard.

Apricots, pawpaw, strawberries, mulberries, etc can all be substituted for peaches and all are delicious.

WATERMELON AND MINT DESSERT (Serves 10)

This to me is a most glorious way of serving watermelon and it is the perfect end to a summer meal.

1 ripe watermelon
500–750 ml (2–3 cups) white sugar
500 ml (2 cups) chopped mint

Cut the melon in half lengthwise, and refrigerate one half. Scoop out all the flesh with a melon scoop or spoon. Discard the pips. Drain the shell, scraping out the last bits of flesh. Mix the sugar with the mint, and blend until crumbly. Just before serving, place a layer of melon balls into the shell and sprinkle with a little mint and sugar mixture. Fill the shell with the rest of the melon balls and top with the mint and sugar mixture. Tuck in sprigs of mint for decoration, place on a silver tray and serve immediately.

Cantaloup and honeydew melons can also be prepared this way.

BRANDIED FRUIT

This is a special treat for Christmas time. I serve it in champagne glasses with whipped cream. It is also delicious with ice-cream.

Ripe red or white grapes (or ripe, firm, unblemished apricots, or ripe, firm, hulled strawberries)

Syrup

4 cups sugar
1 litre (4 cups) water
500 ml (2 cups) lemon verbena leaves or 500 ml (2 cups) bergamot leaves

Boil ingredients for 15–20 minutes. Strain and remove the leaves. Cool.

Prick the fruit with a darning needle. Pack into jars. Mix the syrup with an equal quantity of brandy, pour over the fruit, covering it. Seal well and store for at least 1 month before opening it. Remember – a little goes a long way!

ELDER FLOWER FRITTERS (Serves 6)

Midsummer is the time for the exquisite white elder flowers. I cannot wait to make them into fritters and I relish every mouthful. This is a special occasion treat and I've not met anyone who isn't enchanted to eat flowers this way.

12 heads elder flowers, with stems
250 g (8 oz) flour (I use ½ brown and ½ cake flour)
2 egg whites, well beaten
250 ml (1 cup) warm water or milk
10 ml (2 tsp) baking powder
oil

Whisk together all ingredients, except elder flowers, until smooth. Hold each flower by its stalk and dip into the batter. Fry in hot oil until golden. Drain on crumpled kitchen paper. Snip off the tough stems, dredge with icing sugar and serve with whipped cream. Borage flowers, violets and rose petals can be done in this way too.

CANDIED ANGELICA

This is an unusual herb, at its best in midsummer, and it can be used as a sweet or decoration for cakes, puddings and ice-cream.

angelica stems and leaf ribs
sugar

Slice the angelica stems into 5 cm (2") lengths. Place them in a pan with water and simmer until tender. Lift the stems out of the water and scrape off the bitter outer skin with a knife. Return to the pan and simmer for a few more minutes.

Drain. Weigh the stems. Measure out 150 ml (½ pt) water to each 500 g (1 lb) sugar and pour into a heavy pan. Gradually bring to the boil, stirring well, and boil for 10–20 minutes until the mixture becomes syrupy and thick. Lay the stems in a shallow dish, pour the syrup over them, cover and leave to stand overnight. Next day pour the syrup back into the pan, bring to the boil and again pour over the stems. Leave overnight. Do this twice more, until the syrup is used up and the stems have absorbed it all. Sprinkle with more sugar, and place on a rack to dry out. Store in an airtight tin between layers of greaseproof paper. Use chopped or sliced pieces lavishly on party puddings and cakes.

HERBED ICE-CREAM

Ice-cream is far easier to make than you might think and it is so refreshing on a summer day. Here are two basic recipes which can be adapted to various summer fruits and herbs. You will probably find much pleasure in forming your own particular varieties.

VIOLET ICE-CREAM

1 litre (4 cups) fresh cream
3 eggs, well beaten
250 g (8 oz) sugar (some people prefer castor sugar)
crystallised violets and mint leaves to decorate
750 ml (3 cups) fresh violets

Remove the green calyx from the violet flowers. Warm the cream in a double boiler, mix in the violet flowers, and leave until cold. Then whip the sugar into the cream, fold in the beaten eggs, pour into freezing trays and place in the deep freeze.

Vary this recipe by substituting the following for violets: mint leaves, lemon balm leaves, 500 ml (2 cups) bergamot leaves, 500 ml (2 cups) lemon verbena leaves, 500 ml (2 cups) scented geranium leaves, elder flowers or rose petals. Mince finely.

QUICK FRUIT ICE-CREAM (Serves 6–10)

This ice-cream is very rich and should therefore be served with fruit. It is also an absolutely foolproof ice-cream which will earn you many compliments.

1 litre (4 cups) well-whipped thick cream
1 tin condensed milk
4 cups fruit, eg strawberries, granadillas, mulberries, peaches,
apricots, grated pineapple, youngberries etc.
juice of 1 lemon
mint to decorate
125 ml (½ cup) chopped lemon balm

Mash the fruit well, or if you like it smooth, put through a liquidiser. Blend chopped herbs and lemon juice into the fruit, then pour in the condensed milk. Whisk well. Add the thick, well-whisked cream. Pour into freezer trays and place in the deep freeze.

HERB JELLIES

Jellies are the quickest of all summer puddings and this is a standard way of making a jelly to which fruit can be added. I find peaches, apricots, grated pineapple, granadillas, and strawberries are the nicest. Make your jellies early in the morning so that they are set and cool by lunchtime.

20 g unflavoured gelatine
1 litre (4 cups) boiling water into which 250 ml (1 cup) of herb is
steeped, eg lemon balm (melissa), mint, bergamot, lemon
verbena, scented geranium, lemon thyme
500–750 ml (2–3 cups) sliced fruit, eg peaches, apricots,
strawberries, grapes
250 ml (1 cup) sugar

Dissolve the gelatine in a little of the warm herb tea. Add the sugar and allow it to dissolve. Stir and strain the herb tea. Mix in the fruit and pour into a glass bowl. Place in the refrigerator to set. Decorate with mint leaves and fresh fruit and serve with custard or whipped cream.

NB If you use grated pineapple, cook it first for 5 minutes in its own juice. If used fresh, the acids in it will prevent the jelly from setting.

Breads, Biscuits and Cakes

Baking bread in summer can sometimes be a chore, and I prefer to bake the lighter breads that are quick and easy to prepare. This basic soda bread is delicious when a few chopped herbs are added. My favourites are marjoram, thyme and basil, but oregano, sage, rosemary and dill are also delicious. If you are serving bread with homemade jams, apricot or peach particularly, chop in a few lemon balm, bergamot or scented geranium leaves.

HERBED PAN BREAD

4 cups flour (2 cake flour and 2 wholewheat)
approx 500 ml (2 cups) milk, buttermilk or sour milk
5 ml (1 tsp) salt
20 ml (4 tsp) baking powder
25 ml (2 tbsp) fresh herbs, eg thyme

Sift flour, salt and baking powder. Mix in milk (enough to make a soft dough), add herbs and mix well. Grease a frying pan and heat to medium heat. Put in the dough and spread evenly. Keep heat low. After 10 minutes, lift the bread out onto a plate and grease the pan once more. Turn the bread over and let it cook 10–15 minutes on the other side. Serve hot with butter or dripping.

SAVOURY HERB PASTRIES (Makes about 24)

Light and tasty, these pastries can be used with many herb combinations. They make an excellent accompaniment to summer soups in place of the heavier breads.

500 ml (2 cups) flour
500 ml (2 cups) butter
5 ml (1 tsp) salt
water or milk
125 ml (½ cup) chopped herb, eg parsley, marjoram, lovage,
  basil, oregano, rosemary, sage, mint, thyme.

87

Rub the butter into the flour. Add the chopped herbs. Combine with enough milk or water to make a stiff dough. Roll out to about 1 cm thick and cut into diamonds or squares, or pinch off pieces and roll in the hands and flatten with a fork. Place on a greased baking sheet and bake at 190°C (375°F) for 10 minutes or until light golden.

DATE AND BERGAMOT FRIDGE CAKE

This cake is a marvellous treat and very easy to make. A short cut is to buy a packet of digestive biscuits for the crust. If you have the time, make any plain biscuit to use for the crust, and break up into small pieces. I find this fridge cake an energy giver, and served with iced, unsweetened herb tea, it is an instant success.

500 ml (2 cups) melted butter
250 ml (1 cup) chopped dates
250 ml (1 cup) chopped nuts, eg pecans or almonds
5 ml (1 tsp) vanilla essence
12,5–25 ml (1–2 tbsp) finely chopped bergamot leaves (or mint or lemon balm)
1 full packet digestive biscuits
2–3 eggs

88

Melt butter and sugar over medium heat. Whisk eggs and whisk into butter and sugar mixture. Chop and melt the dates in a little butter over medium heat. Add to egg and butter and sugar mixture. Add chopped herbs. Break biscuits into fairly small pieces (do not crumble) and fold into the date mixture. Mix well. Grease a cake tin or dish very well, or line with heavy-duty tinfoil. Press the mixture into the tin and place it in the refrigerator for 5 hours. Cut up into squares and serve with herb tea.

MERINGUES WITH HERB CREAM

For a summer afternoon tea party, nothing beats a homemade meringue. Add some whipped cream spiced with herbs and it makes an excellent party sweet or dessert. Decorate with mint leaves and candied fruit.

2–3 egg whites
1 breakfast cup white sugar
10 ml (2 level tsp) baking powder

Whisk egg whites with a pinch of salt until they form stiff peaks. Gradually add in half the sugar, sprinkling in a little at a time and whisking continuously. Stir the baking powder into the rest of the sugar and mix well. Fold into the whisked eggs and sugar. Instead of using a baking tray, fold 3 or 4 sheets of newspaper to fit the oven shelf. Place spoonfuls of meringue evenly spaced on the paper. Bake at 100°C (220°F) for several hours. I usually leave them overnight or until the meringue is brittle and dry. Store in airtight tins.

Herb Cream

250 ml (1 cup) heavy cream
60 ml (½ cup) milk
25 ml (2 tbsp) icing sugar
25 ml (2 tbsp) chopped herb, eg mint, lemon balm, lemon thyme,
  bergamot, elder flowers, violets, rose petals

Whisk cream and milk. Add the icing sugar and the chopped herb. Whisk together well. Take 2 meringues and press together with a spoonful of the cream. Place in paper cups, or on small plates and decorate with mint, rosemary or a sprinkling of chopped almonds.

CRYSTALLISED FLOWERS OR LEAVES

Simple to make, crystallised flowers and leaves can transform even the plainest pudding or cake into a party piece.

1 egg white, beaten
several violets, mint leaves, rose petals, lemon balm leaves, borage
flowers or violet leaves
castor sugar

Beat the egg white with a fork until it is opaque but not foamy and stiff. The leaves and flowers must be completely dry. Dip each into the egg white, turning until it is completely coated. Sprinkle with castor sugar, again making sure that it is thoroughly coated. (If you want a lavender flavour submerge lavender flowers in the sugar for a few days before using.) Lay the coated leaves and flowers on greaseproof paper. Dry in a very cool oven, leaving the door half open, or place in the hot sun. When completely dry and brittle store in an airtight tin. Use to decorate cakes, puddings and ice-cream.

Drinks

A cool drink need no longer mean a glass of lemonade or squeezed orange juice. Today a variety of iced teas and herb cocktails are at your fingertips. Experiment with combinations of herbs and fruits for refreshing, cooling and invigorating summer drinks.

HERB TEAS

Plain herb teas form the basis for a huge variety of flavours, and are healthy and energy giving. Listed below are my own favourite herbs which I use for cold teas, fruit punches and syrups. Even served alone as a tea, with a little lemon juice, a teaspoon or two of honey and an ice cube, each one is delicious. Vary the strength by adding more or less of your chosen herb. Try the following – bergamot, lemon balm, lavender, scented geranium, lemon verbena, elder flowers, rosemary, lemon thyme, and the mints (peppermint, spearmint etc). I usually work to a proportion of 60 ml (¼ cup) herb to 250 ml (1 cup) boiling water. Stand, steep and cool. If you are adding fruit juice, 125 ml (½ cup) herb to 250 ml (1 cup) boiling water is ideal, adding 250 ml (1 cup) fruit juice (eg granadilla, pine-apple, apple, peach, pear, or grape). Sweeten if you like and add a few mint leaves for decoration.

STANDARD HERB PUNCH (Serves 6–10)

1 litre (4 cups) unsweetened, unpreserved fruit juice, eg granadilla
1 litre (4 cups) strong herb tea – made by pouring 1 litre (4 cups)
*   boiling water over 4 cups mint or rosemary twigs*
37,5 ml (3 tbsp) honey
juice of 2 lemons
pulp of 4 or 5 granadillas
little chopped pineapple

Cool the herb tea. Strain and discard the herbs. Stir in the honey until well dissolved and mixed. Add the fruit juice, granadilla pulp and the chopped pineapple. Pour into glass jugs. Place in the refrigerator to chill. Just before serving, add a few ice cubes and the mint leaves.

HERB FRUIT WINE CUP (Serves 20)

This is a party drink, wonderfully refreshing and festive. The nicest fruits to use are strawberries or soft ripe peaches, but I have also made it most successfully with lychees. White grapes, popped from their skins, are delicious too, so experiment with whatever fruit you have on hand. Make notes as you go along – it can be frustrating if you wish to repeat a memorable wine cup and can't remember the exact quantities you used!

2 bottles sweet white wine
1 litre (4 cups) soda water
2 sprigs each of fresh mint, sage,
  rosemary and lemon verbena
5–10 scented geranium leaves
  (I find rose geranium best)
4 cups fresh, hulled strawberries
  (or sliced peaches, peeled and
  de-pipped, or litchis or grapes)
50 ml (4 tbsp) honey
fresh geranium leaves for decoration

Lightly crush the herbs and place in a large jar. Pour the wine over the herbs. Steep for 3–4 hours at room temperature. Crush the strawberries with a fork, drizzle with the honey, and place in the refrigerator for 3–4 hours. Add the honeyed strawberries to the wine. Chill well. Serve in a punch bowl, placing it in a larger bowl filled with crushed ice. At the last minute, stir in the soda water. Float small scented geranium leaves on top for that final touch.

HERB SYRUP

This is a quick and easy herb syrup base, ready to be diluted with either a herb tea, with fruit juice or even plain water. Several herbs lend themselves to this: lavender, rosemary, the mints, lemon verbena, lemon balm, bergamot, scented geranium and elder flowers, rose petals and violets. I like to combine two or three herbs.

½ litre (2 cups) lemon juice
½ litre (2 cups) water
½–1 litre (2–4 cups) sugar
4 cups herb, eg lemon verbena and mint

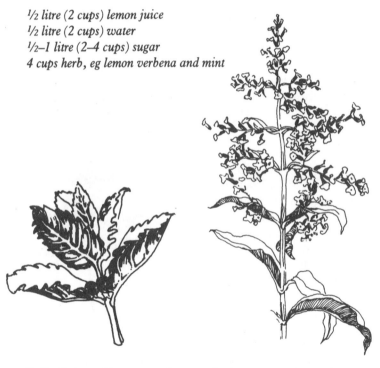

Boil all ingredients together gently in a covered pot for 10 minutes. Remove from the heat, stand, steep and cool. Strain out the herbs, bottle and store in the refrigerator. Use by diluting with cold herb teas or fruit juices – eg 60 ml (¼ cup) syrup to 1 large cup juice or tea. Serve with ice, a twist of lemon peel and a mint leaf or two on top.

HERB MILK PICK-ME-UP

If you have had an exhausting day this effective energy restorer is quick and easy to make. It revitalises and cools, and is wonderfully sustaining.

1 glass chilled milk
1 egg
2 ml (½ tsp) powdered ginger
10–20 ml (2–4 tsp) finely chopped rosemary
pinch nutmeg
12,5 ml (1 tbsp) honey

Whisk all ingredients together in a liquidiser. Pour into a glass and drink immediately. Add a little more honey if you have a sweet tooth.

TOMATO JUICE WITH HERBS (Serves 4–6)

This is a savoury drink that is wonderfully refreshing and nourishing. Add some carrot juice and it is a meal in itself. Once again this is a basic recipe and other fruits can be added. Try using pineapple, herbs like sorrel, comfrey, borage, salad burnet, watercress, and vegetables such as cucumber, celery, radish, or sugar snap peas (uncooked).

4 large ripe tomatoes
25 ml (2 tbsp) fresh basil
25 ml (2 tbsp) fresh lemon juice
250 ml (1 cup) watercress
12,5 ml (1 tbsp) parsley
250 ml (1 cup) herb stock or tea (eg celery tea made by pouring
    250 ml (1 cup) boiling water over 60–125 ml (¼–½ cup)
    chopped celery. Stand 10 minutes. Strain.)
salt and pepper to taste

Place all ingredients in a liquidiser and blend well. Serve in individual glasses, topped with sprigs of watercress.

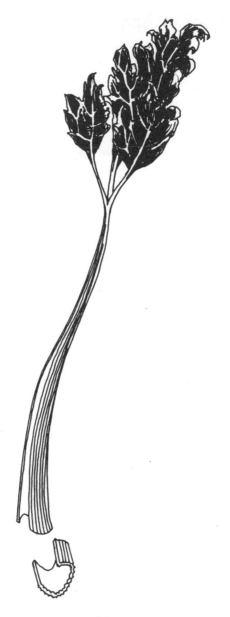